To Granny

Christmas   1983

Acknowledgements

The publishers gratefully acknowledge permission to reprint copyright material from the following:
'Our England is a Garden,' four lines from **The Glory of the Garden**, page 12, and 'The cure for this ill is not to sit still,' four lines from 'Sing-Song of Old Man Kangaroo' from **The Just So Stories**, page 80, both by Rudyard Kipling, reprinted by permission of the National Trust and Macmillan, London Limited; recipes for Rose Petal Vinegar, Potpourri, Rhubarb and Elderflower Jam, Elderflower 'Champagne,' Preserved Nasturtium Seeds, Crab Apple Jelly, Rose and Perfumed Jellies, Jelly Making Hints and Japonica Jam taken from **The Country Housewife's Handbook** published by and obtainable from Kent-West Kent Federation of Women's Institutes, Hunt House, 64 College Road, Maidstone, Kent, ME15 6SW; 'As butterflies are but winged flowers,' four lines from **The Ways of Time**, page 58, by William Henry Davies reprinted by permission of the Executors of the Estate of W. H. Davies and Jonathan Cape Limited; extract from **Loveliest of trees, the cherry now**, page 22, by A. E. Housman reprinted by permission of The Society of Authors as the literary representative of the Estate of A. E. Housman, and Jonathan Cape Ltd., publishers of A. E. Housman's **Collected Poems**.
The publishers have made every effort to trace the copyright holders. If we have inadvertently omitted to acknowledge anyone we should be most grateful if this could be brought to our attention for correction at the first opportunity.

British library cataloguing in publication data

Barker, Cicely Mary
The flower fairies gardening year.
1. Gardening
I. Title
635   SB450.97

ISBN 0-216-91480-9

Printed in Great Britain

The Flower Fairies
GARDENING YEAR

with illustrations by
Cicely Mary Barker
Foreword by
Percy Thrower

Blackie

Contents

Foreword

I am fortunate that gardening is not only my living but my hobby as well, one that provides me with relaxation and a sense of achievement. Gardening is the most popular hobby in Britain at the present time and I am always anxious that others should get the same enjoyment from their gardens as I get from mine. There are more than 17 million homes with gardens in Britain and more than a thousand million pounds is spent on these gardens every year – a lot of gardens and a lot of money. If we can help these millions of garden owners to get value for the money they spend and value for the effort they put in, then we have done a worthwhile job.

The secret of a good garden is continuity of colour and interest the year round, and this is possible, as this useful little book explains, even in the smallest of gardens. The garden of today is one which is more or less permanently planted with trees, shrubs, roses and hardy border plants, more costly in the initial outlay but a big saving in time and money in the long run. A permanently planted garden can have colour and interest throughout the year by careful selection of shrubs and other plants.

The most important part of the garden to me is the lawn. If the lawn looks good the rest of the garden looks so much better. This is well catered for in the chapters of this book. There is information on the care of roses, too. More roses are planted in British gardens than any other flower I could mention, and what better for continual flowering from June to November? They are permanent and keep the recurring work down to a minimum.

This book is easy and enjoyable to read, helpful in all seasons. It is written in simple, down-to-earth terms with good practical advice for beginners and for those who have been gardening for a number of years. I hope that you will enjoy it as much as I have done and that it will help you to get the best from your garden. Your immediate surroundings will be more beautiful and if others follow your example the whole of the British Isles will be an even more beautiful place to live in.

Percy Thrower

SPRING

It was a lover and his lass,
  With a hey, and a ho, and a hey nonino,
That o'er the green cornfield did pass,
  In the spring time, the only pretty ring time,
When birds do sing, hey ding a ding, ding;
  Sweet lovers love the spring.
William Shakespeare

Spring is the season for surprises in the garden; delicate green shoots appear overnight from winter-hardened soil, buds begin to swell, and the first flowers of the year provide patches of bright colour. Primulas, for example, come into their own at this time of year, when there is no competition from other bedding plants.

Early shrubs, including Japonica, Flowering Currants and Forsythia are a mass of flowers, and spring bulbs – Crocuses, Daffodils, Anemones, Scillas and Grape Hyacinths – relieve the winter gloom. In April, Rhododendrons and Azaleas are ablaze with shocking pink, crimson, purple and orange flowers.

It is the busiest time of year for the gardener: preparing the soil, planting new trees and shrubs, sowing seeds and planning ahead for the rest of the year. The longer, milder days prove an incentive to even the most reluctant gardener. Now is the time to abandon the comfortable fireside chair and start digging!

SCILLA

Jobs in Your Garden in Spring

Our England is a garden, and such
gardens are not made
By singing: – 'Oh, how beautiful!' and
sitting in the shade,
While better men than we go out and
start their working lives
At grubbing weeds from gravel paths
with broken dinner knives.
Rudyard Kipling

The Lawn

Rake the lawn to remove dead grass and other rubbish, and to let
light, air and moisture reach the roots. In March, when the ground is
firm after a dry spell and the grass is about two inches high, it's time
to mow the lawn for the first time and to neaten up the edges. Raise
the mower's blades for the first mowing. By the time April comes you
will probably need to mow twice a week and this will be your routine
for the rest of the spring and summer. Apply a spring fertiliser,
following the manufacturer's instructions with great care.

Annuals

Make your final choice of seeds from a catalogue or garden centre.
When the soil begins to warm up – by the end of March in the south
– the ground can be prepared for the first sowing of hardy annuals
(see pages 20 and 34). In May, you can plant annual seedlings. Water
the seedlings and the ground before planting, to give them a good
start. It's helpful, also, to lay out all the seedlings on the ground
where you plan to plant them. Then you can see whether your
planting plan is going to work and make sure that the plants will be
evenly spaced.

Bulbs

By the end of March most of your Daffodils will have finished
flowering. Remove the dead flower heads to encourage the plants to
put all their energy into plumping out the bulbs for next year. Don't
cut off the leaves. Leave the seed heads on Snowdrops, Crocuses and
Scillas if you would like them to seed themselves and spread. Bulbs
grown indoors for Christmas can now be planted out in the garden.
They will need a year or two to recover from being 'forced'.

Roses

Many gardeners prune their Roses in March (see page 40 for instructions). Apply a special Rose fertiliser now, or add a mulch to the surrounding soil with manure, garden compost, moistened peat or grass cuttings. From late spring onwards it's wise to spray your Roses frequently to protect them from aphids, mildew, black spot and rust. If suckers appear, cut them off below the surface of the soil, at the point where they join a root.

The Herbaceous Border

If you have taken over a well-established garden you may already have a border of hardy, colourful perennials which will require very little work. In March and April they will show their first signs of new growth after the winter. New perennials can be planted now, for instance Lupins, Delphiniums, or Pyrethrums (brightly coloured daisy-like flowers which are ideal for cutting).

Hoe the border to get rid of the weeds which will be appearing now. In April, the tall shoots of Delphiniums will need to be supported with stakes or canes. Use twiggy pea sticks to support Pinks and Pyrethrums. May is the time to plant out Chrysanthemums and Dahlias in the border.

Diary for March

March brings breezes loud and shrill,
Stirs the dancing daffodil.

CROCUS

Diary for April

April brings the primrose sweet,
Scatters daisies at our feet.

Diary for May

May brings flocks of pretty lambs,
Skipping by their fleecy dams.

Bulbs

However grey and miserable the weather may be in February and March, early-flowering bulbs such as Snowdrops and Crocuses bring a promise that spring really is on the way.

Here are some bulbs for you to enjoy in spring and early summer, and a few more unusual ones to introduce a little variety.

Daffodils and *Narcissi* belong to the same family (narcissus is the family name). They are easy to grow in borders, in areas of short grass which won't need mowing too early in the year, or on banks, and they make excellent cut flowers. There are innumerable varieties, from the familiar yellow daffodil with its trumpet-shaped flower to double-flowered, pure white, gold and white, orange and white, or miniature daffodils. The miniatures look particularly good in a rockery.

To edge a border, you can choose from a number of smaller bulbs. *Snowdrops* are best planted where they will not be disturbed and can seed themselves to make thicker clumps year by year. They have either single or double flowers. *Crocuses* usually like a sunny position. The sunshine encourages their flowers to open out. Don't forget that there are autumn-flowering varieties, too. *Grape Hyacinths* also look good in a rockery and like to be in the sun. There is a white variety as well as the more familiar dark blue. Perhaps the bluest flower of all is the dainty *Scilla.* Plant it in clumps for the best effect.

For a scented garden in spring, try *Lily of the Valley* and *Hyacinth. Lily of the Valley* likes a moist, semi-shaded position. Its sweet-smelling flowers are borne in April and May. *Hyacinth,* a favourite for growing indoors, bears its blue, pink, purple, white or yellow flowers out of doors in March and April, or indoors in time for Christmas.

Tulips may make you think of formal town parks or gardens where you see them planted in regimented rows, but they will provide welcome colour from April onwards when the earlier bulbs have faded and your summer bedding plants are not yet in flower. Try planting them in informal groups mixed with Wallflowers and Forget-me-nots.

Two of the more unusual bulbs which you might like to try are *Alliums* and *Fritillaries.* The stately *Crown Imperial* with its straight, sturdy stem and cluster of bright orange, red or yellow pendant flowers, belongs to the Fritillary family, although it looks quite unlike the intriguing *Snake's Head Fritillary,* which has delicately chequered flowers in shades or purple and white or green and white. *Alliums* belong to the same family as onions, leeks and chives.and have an oniony smell. Many of them bear brightly coloured balls of flowers and they mostly flower from June onwards.

NARCISSUS

Soil and its Preparation

He digs the flowers, green, red, and blue,
Nor wishes to be spoken to.
He digs the flowers and cuts the hay,
And never seems to want to play.
Robert Louis Stevenson

Digging and raking may feel 'back breaking' at the time, but the hard work is well worth the effort. Provided you know a few basic facts about the soil in your garden, you can avoid making expensive mistakes and ensure that your plants are healthy and happy.

What is Soil?

All soil is made up of rock particles, water, air and humus (decayed plant and animal material). The layer of soil on the surface is known as *top soil*. It is composed mainly of humus and earth. Under the topsoil lies the *subsoil*. The two must never be mixed and subsoil should not be put on top of the topsoil.

Acid or Alkaline?

An inexpensive soil testing kit will tell you whether your soil is mainly alkaline (limy) or acid. Azaleas, Rhododendrons, Camellias and Primulas hate lime and only do well on an acid soil.

Chalky soils are alkaline and peat is acid. The best soil has a good balance of the two, with just a little more acid than alkaline. Don't despair if you find you have a problem soil, as it can be remedied by adding whatever is missing, though this may take some time, and a lot of effort!

Texture

Some soils are heavy and sticky, others are light and grainy. Clay is a good example of a very sticky soil, and sand is particularly light. Both can be improved by the addition of compost, manure or other organic mixtures. You can buy these at a garden centre and the information on the packet will lead you to the best one for your soil.

Digging

If you have a huge area of soil to dig, a mechanical cultivator is probably the answer. Otherwise, you will have to roll up your sleeves and use a spade. Autumn is the best time to turn the soil over. Don't dig too deep, just one spade head's depth is the right amount.

Winter frosts help to break the soil up further, and in spring you can finish the job off with a rake, leaving a fine tilth.

Digging improves the aeration of the soil, making it easier for roots to breathe, and it allows rain water to filter through. It also helps to keep weeds under control.

Sowing Seeds

We plough the fields, and scatter
The good seed on the land,
But it is fed and watered
By God's Almighty Hand.
Jane Montgomery Campbell

Early spring is the time to sow seeds to ensure a colourful summer display. By March, the soil is beginning to warm up. Winter frosts will have done their work in breaking up the larger lumps, and a good raking and sieving should give a fine tilth.

There are two methods for raising plants from seed: under glass and in the open ground. The instructions on the seed packet will tell you which method to use and how long the seeds will take to germinate. READ THE INSTRUCTIONS CAREFULLY.

Seeds need ***warmth, water*** and ***air,*** but they do not react kindly to over-watering or too much direct heat. Be careful not to sow seeds too deeply or too thickly.

Sowing Under Glass

1. Fill a clean seed tray with compost to within about half an inch of the top.

2. Sow seeds finely and sprinkle a thin layer of compost over.

3. Water lightly using a 'rose' or plant spray.

4. Cover seed tray with a polythene bag or a piece of glass.

5. Place a sheet of brown paper on top to speed up germination.

6. Remove paper as soon as seedlings appear. The glass or polythene bag can be left on for another couple of days.

7. When the seedlings have four or more leaves, gently prick them out into a new tray.

8. Water seedlings regularly and keep in a warm, shady spot.

9. Some seedlings may need to be 'hardened' off in a cold frame. Others can be planted out immediately.

Mark out a shallow drill.

Shake seeds carefully along drill.

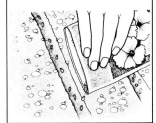

Lightly cover with soil.

Mark with labels.

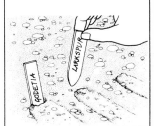

Thin out weaker seedlings.

Flowering Trees

To provide a focal point in your garden in spring, what could be better than a flowering tree? With careful planning you can choose a selection of trees to give you a display of blossom from March until June.

One of the earliest ornamental trees to flower is the **Blackthorn**. It has a mass of delicate white flowers in March and in the autumn you can use its fruit to flavour sloe gin. Another early bloomer is ***Prunus Pissardii,*** whose pale pink flowers are borne in February and March and come showering down before the dark purplish-brown leaves open out.

Almonds bear their showy pink flowers on bare branches in March and April. Although the flowers are lovely, don't hope for edible nuts. Our climate is just too cold!

Magnolia Soulangiana is one of the most popular magnolias. It has elegant, tulip-shaped flowers which are white with a pink flush at the base of the petals. It flowers from March to April. Magnolias need to be grown in a sheltered spot, away from chilly winter winds, or their flower buds may be damaged by frost.

Cherries can be grown for ornament as well as fruit. The Japanese pink, double-flowered cherry is almost too popular in surburban and public gardens, but deservedly so. In the second half of April it is covered in flowers, and these are followed by attractive copper coloured young leaves which turn to green in the summer.

The ***Crab Apple*** is now grown mainly for the sake of its very decorative flowers, but you can make a delicious jelly with its fruit. The variety ***Malus Floribunda*** flowers in May. The flower buds are deep pink and the petals fade to a paler pink as they open.

Lilac is a good choice for a town garden, where it will thrive. The mauve or white flowers with their delicious scent come out in May and June.

LILAC

Growing Herbs

'There's Rosemary; that's for remembrance.'
William Shakespeare

Herbs are among the most rewarding plants in the garden. They are easily grown and require a minimum of attention. You can use them as flavouring in cooking, for medicinal purposes, as cosmetics and for their fresh, sweet smelling aroma.

Many gardeners, not rating herbs as 'proper plants', relegate a few popular varieties to a neglected part of the garden where they soon run wild. Then the unfortunate gardener wonders why the 'herb garden' looks so untidy! But herbs can grow quite happily alongside other plants in borders and beds. Many have brightly-coloured flowers and attractive foliage. And they smell wonderful.

The art of growing herbs successfully is to think carefully before planting. Find out how large the plant is likely to become and how far it will spread. Some are extremely difficult to tame – Mint is a good example. Others, such as Rosemary and Bay, grow into large bushes.

A popular device for keeping herbs in check is to plant different varieties between the spokes of an old wooden wheel.

You don't have to have a garden to grow herbs. They will grow quite happily in a window box, or in pots in the kitchen. Many nurseries sell young plants in pots, which saves you waiting for seeds to come up.

The following are some useful herbs to grow. The first measurement is the approximate height of a mature plant, and the second is a guide to how far it is likely to spread.

Chives (6 in. x 18 in.) Sow seeds in spring and again in early autumn. The green stems have a strong oniony flavour and are delicious when finely chopped over salads and soups. Plants die down in winter but grow again the following year.

Bay (15 ft.) Take cuttings from an existing plant in August. Or, buy a young plant from a nursery (mature Bays are extremely expensive). Plant in a sheltered, sunny position. Leaves have a strong aroma and can be used fresh or dried. Add to soups, stews and meat dishes.

D*ill* (5 ft. x 2 ft.) Sow seeds end March in well-drained soil. Delicate, feathery leaves are ideal for flavouring fish dishes. Soak seeds in vinegar to make Dill vinegar.

F*ennel* (12 in.) Sow seeds in May. Leaves have strong aniseed aroma. The flavour goes well with fish and cheese dishes and salads.

M*arjoram* (12 in.) Sow seeds in March in a sunny position. There are two main varieties: pot Marjoram (perennial) and wild Marjoram, also a perennial, and sometimes known as Oregano. Adds flavour to meat and fish and poultry, pizzas and pasta sauces.

M*int* (12 in. x infinity!) Plant in moist, shaded spot. Grows prolifically. To check growth, sink a bottomless bucket in the soil before planting. This will restrict the roots. Divide roots in March. Use chopped leaves for making mint sauce or jelly to accompany roast lamb.

T*hyme* (10 in.) Sow seeds in April, ideally in dry, chalky soil. Add to savoury dishes, such as *Mushroom à la Grecque.*

T*arragon* (Russian 5 ft.: French 3 ft.) French Tarragon has a much better flavour. Buy plant from a reputable nursery. Use in savoury dishes and for making Tarragon vinegar.

P*arsley* (9 in. x 6 in.) Sow seeds in March-April in a sunny position. Germination is slow. Superstition has it that if you sow the seeds on Good Friday they do not have to go down to the Devil and back! Often used to decorate savoury dishes, and for making delicious Parsley sauce.

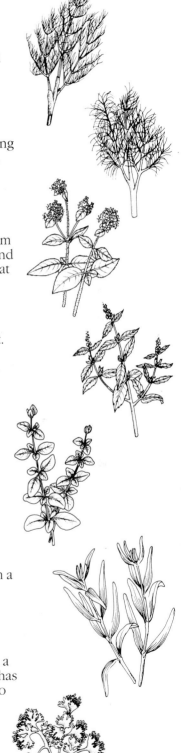

SUMMER

Rough winds do shake the darling buds of May,
And Summer's lease hath all too short a date.
William Shakespeare

During the hot summer months there will be plenty of time to sit back and enjoy the results of all your hard work in the garden – though there are still quite a few jobs to do!

Summer annuals in all the colours of the rainbow fill borders and rock gardens. Window boxes and hanging baskets are a mass of colour. Even if you don't have a garden, you can still create a bright display by using flower pots, tubs and grow-bags.

If you haven't had the time or space to raise your own plants, you can achieve an 'instant' garden by visiting your local garden centre. Most garden centres and nurseries sell boxes of young plants, which you can very quickly plant in your garden, or in tubs.

Some of the most popular summer flowers are: Alyssum, Antirrhinums (snap-dragons), Asters, Begonias, Dahlias, Delphiniums, Gypsophilas, Sunflowers, Lilies, Lobelia, Stock, Poppies, Roses, Salvia, Sedum, Marigolds, Verbena and many more.

Summer is a good time to visit other gardens. Many well-known gardens are open to the public. You can pick up useful ideas and some gardens have plants for sale.

PINKS

Jobs in Your Garden in Summer

Sumer is icumen in
Lhude sing cuccu!
Groweth sed, and bloweth med,
And springeth the wude nu.
Cuckoo song *(c. 1250)*

The Lawn

Your lawn will need mowing once or twice a week throughout the summer. To prevent damage in periods of drought give it a good watering, always in the cool of the evening or the morning, never in the middle of a hot, sunny day. To help the water soak in, aerate the lawn once or twice during the summer by pushing in the prongs of a fork to a depth of 3-4 inches at regular intervals of 6-9 inches.

Annuals

Newly-planted annuals will need to be watered during dry spells. Weed the flower bed regularly. To encourage the plants to keep on producing new flowers, cut off all the dead flower heads.

Biennials

Biennials are plants raised from seed one year to flower the next. By thinking ahead and sowing seeds of Sweet Williams, Foxgloves, Forget-me-nots, Canterbury Bells and Wallflowers (strictly speaking perennials) during these summer months you can plan for lots of colour in the flower border in spring and early summer next year, before the annuals come into flower. Sow the seeds in the border or, if you have space, in a separate nursery bed for planting out in September.

Bulbs

July is the month to plant autumn-flowering bulbs such as the Autumn Crocus; and Daffodils should be planted by the end of August if possible. Start making your selection of other spring-flowering bulbs from catalogues or garden shops.

Tulip bulbs should be lifted from the ground after the leaves have turned yellow. Put them in a box in an airy place until they are dry. Then cut off the dead leaves and roots and store the bulbs in a cool, dry place. Any diseased bulbs should be burned.

Roses

Continue spraying to protect Roses from pests, and hoe between bushes to keep weeds at bay. When the flowers have faded, cut them off, making a clean cut just above a leaf. The dead heads should be burned, not put on the compost heap.

The Herbaceous Border

Cut back plants which have finished flowering. In early June, pinch out the tips of Dahlias and Chrysanthemums to encourage them to become more bushy and produce more flowers. They will be growing tall now and will need to be supported. Many plants in the border such as Paeonies, Lilies and Irises, will benefit from having their dead flower heads removed.

General

As the weather warms up, so will your struggle against weeds, pests and diseases. Be ready to spend some time wielding a hoe, insecticide and fungicide sprays during the summer.

Diary for June

June brings tulips, lilies, roses,
Fills the children's hands with posies

FORGET-ME-NOT

Diary for July

Hot July brings cooling showers,
Apricots and gilly flowers.

Diary for August

August brings the sheaves of corn,
Then the harvest home is borne.

Hardy Annuals

A border full of annuals will bring a mass of colour to your garden in midsummer. Many varieties are easy to grow and can be sown directly where you want them to flower. If you prefer to plant them as seedlings, you'll need to wait until early May when all danger of frost has passed.

Annuals like well-drained, well-dug soil and lots of sunshine and air. Because they are so colourful and sturdy, most are excellent for cutting for flower arrangements, bouquets and posies. To achieve the most colourful and dramatic effect, plant them in large clumps.

Here are some favourites for you to enjoy in your garden in summer. You'll find general instructions on soil preparation and sowing seeds on pages 20 and 21.

Alyssum makes a lovely edging for the front of your border with its drifts of white, pink or purple flowers. In formal displays white Alyssum is often combined with dark blue Lobelia. It grows 3-6 inches high and spreads 8-12 inches. It likes a sunny position and flowers from June to September. Sow in March or April.

Candytuft is dainty but colourful, with clusters of pink, mauve or white flowers. It grows 6-15 inches high. It likes a sunny position and if the seeds are sown successively from March until May will give you a good display of flowers all summer long, from May until September. Remove the dead heads and you'll encourage even more flowers to grow. Candytuft is a tolerant plant and will put up with a poor soil and the grimy conditions of a city garden.

CANDYTUFT

Godetia has clusters of single or double flowers in shades of red, pink or white. The dwarf and the 'azalea-flowered' varieties grow 12-15 inches high. It likes sunshine and a light soil, and it flowers from June to August. Sow in March, April or September.

Gypsophila bears a cloud of small, white, pink or red flowers and adds a lacy touch to your garden border or flower arrangements. It grows to 24 inches high, likes a sunny position and is easy to grow. Sow in March, April or September.

Larkspur is a member of the Delphinium family. Its spikes of pink, white or blue flowers are good for cutting. It likes a sunny position, sheltered from the wind. As it grows up to 4 feet tall, it may need to be supported with pea sticks. It flowers from June to September. Sow in September and protect the seedlings from frost during the winter.

Love-in-a-mist has delicate blue, pink or white flowers in a 'mist' of feathery foliage. The pale brown seed pods are very decorative too. It likes sunshine and grows to 24 inches high. Sow in March, April or September.

N*asturtium* with its red, yellow or orange trumpet-shaped flowers and broad, circular leaves is a very familiar plant. It can be grown in tubs and hanging baskets, or in a sunny spot in the garden. It thrives in poor soil. Too rich a soil may make it produce such a luxuriant growth of leaves that the flowers are hidden away. Sadly, blackflies love Nasturtiums, so they are not ideal for a garden where vegetables are grown. The seeds can be preserved in vinegar for use in piquant sauces (see page 49). Sow in April and May for flowers in July, August and September.

P*oppies*   The Shirley Poppy has single flowers, like a wild poppy, or double. The flowers are in pretty shades of pink, white or red. It is a tall plant, suitable for the back of the border, growing to about 24 inches high. It flowers from June to September. Sow in March, April or September.

Roses

No garden would be complete without roses. There are varieties to suit all tastes and all sizes and shapes of gardens. They make excellent cut flowers and a bouquet of roses is still one of the most romantic of gifts.

The marvellous but baffling array of different roses now available to gardeners is descended from species growing in the wild in the Northern Hemisphere. The most direct descendants of these 'Species' roses are the 'Old Roses'. Both tend to be sweetly scented and more resistant to disease than some of the newer varieties, although their flowering period may be shorter. Many also have decorative hips which can make an attractive addition to autumn flower and foliage arrangements.

Most often grown nowadays are the *Hybrid Tea* and *Floribunda* roses. Hybrid Teas have large blooms growing singly on sturdy bushes. Most, but not all, are scented. An ever-popular example is *Peace,* an especially vigorously growing rose with yellow petals shading to pink at the tips. The blooms of *Floribundas* grow in clusters. *Climbers* and *Ramblers* are roses which need to be supported. *Climbers* are generally suitable for growing against a cottage wall or garden fence. They are sturdier than Ramblers and have larger blooms. *Ramblers* can make a lovely low hedge. A good example is *Albertine,* with copious double pink scented flowers.

Miniatures suit small patio gardens and window boxes. They grow to about 9 inches, are hardy and almost thornless.

Standard roses are Hybrid Teas or Floribundas 'budded' onto strong, straight brier stems about 4 feet high. *Weeping Standards* are Ramblers similarly treated. Both need to be supported by strong stakes, driven into the ground before the rose is planted, and Weeping Standards are generally trained over an umbrella-shaped frame of wire hoops.

Growing Roses

Roses can be grown in most types of soil, except very sandy or very chalky soil or very sticky clay. They prefer an open, sunny position with good drainage. To encourage them to produce their best possible blooms they will need lots of watering, particularly in spells of dry summer weather, and annual feeding with chemical fertilisers or bone meal or well-rotted compost or manure. Mulching helps to keep the rose bed moist, to improve the soil and to smother weeds. This is done by covering the surface of the soil around each rose bush with a layer of compost, manure, leaf mould, peat or lawn clippings. (But never use lawn clippings if you have recently treated the lawn with a weedkiller). It's best to put on the mulch when the soil is moist.

ROSE

Pests and Diseases

Sadly, many roses, particularly some modern varieties are susceptible to disease and you will need to protect and treat them carefully.

Miniature

Greenfly congregate on young stems and flower buds. They suck the sap and cover leaves and flowers in a sticky substance. 'Systemic' insecticide, sprayed onto the plants or watered into the soil around the rose bush will enter the sap and kill the greenfly as they suck the sap for the three or four weeks after application.

Shrub

Black Spot first appears as brownish-black spots on healthy-looking leaves. Then the leaves turn yellow and fall.

Mildew is a powdery white coating on leaves. Both are treated by spraying repeatedly with fungicide.

Pruning: making a sloping cut above an outward facing bud.

Pruning

Pruning is an important part of the care of your roses. It improves the shape of the rose bush and encourages strong new growth.
Below are some guidelines on how to prune your roses. Most pruning is done in March and early April, preferably in a mild spell to avoid frost damage to the cut stems.

Species and Old Roses Very little pruning is needed, but remove dead or weak stems and cut back any that have become over-long.

Hybrid Teas Remove all dead wood and weak growths and cut back to about four or six inches above the ground, above an outward-facing bud. This should leave two or three buds on each stem.

Standard

Floribundas As Hybrid Teas, but leave about four or five buds on each stem.

Climbers Cut back lateral stems, but leave the main upright stems unless they have become unmanageably long.

Weeping Standard

Ramblers have usually finished flowering by the end of the summer and can be cut back when all the flowers have faded. Prune the stems which have just flowered right down to the ground. Next year's best flowers will be carried on this year's new growth.

Always burn all trimmings to prevent diseases from recurring. Never put them on the compost heap. Two other jobs that will need to be done regularly are the removal of dead heads, which encourages new flowers, and the removal of suckers. Most roses are 'budded' onto the root of another species, such as a brier. Shoots growing from these roots are suckers. They usually look greener and thornier than other shoots and should be cut or wrenched away from the point where they join the root *below* the surface of the soil.

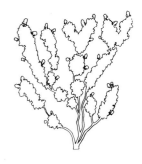

Climber

Preserving Flowers

It is possible to have colourful flower arrangements in the house all year round – even when there is snow on the ground and frost in the air. And it need not cost a penny! Flowers, leaves and grasses cut in spring and summer can be preserved for use throughout the year. And 'everlasting' flowers really do last for ever.

Preserved flowers can be used in many ways: for making potpourri, Lavender bags, and pressed flower pictures and cards. All of these make wonderfully inexpensive, attractive gifts.

It is not difficult to treat plant material to make it last for ever. But there are a few golden rules.

* Summer is the best time to harvest flowers, and grasses. Pick them when they are in peak condition. Everlasting flowers should be picked before the flowers are fully open.

* Always pick material when it is dry, or it may rot during the drying-out process.

* Take great care not to damage flower heads when picking.

* Remove broken and mis-shapen leaves.

Air Drying

Air drying

This is the easiest method for preserving many flowers, grasses and herbs including 'everlasting' flowers. It usually takes 2 to 4 weeks. There are a few important do's and don't's.

1. Choose a drying area that is warm, dry and dark. For example, a large airing cupboard, or near a central heating boiler.

2. Hang long, heavy stems individually, supporting with wire if necessary. Small flowers and grasses can be lightly bunched together. All flowers should be hung with their heads down.

3. Handle very carefully. Dried plant material is very fragile.

LAVENDER

Plant Material for Drying

S*eedheads* - Honesty, Chinese Lantern, Poppy, Pussy
Willow

G*rasses* - Pampas Grass, Wheat, Barley, Rye, Quaking
Grass, Bulrush

F*lowers* - Lavender, Delphinium, Shrub Rose, Iris,
Love-in-a-mist

E*verlasting Flowers* - Straw Daisy, Sand Flower,
Spanish Cloves, Sea Lavender, Sea Holly, African Daisy

Drying with a Dessicant

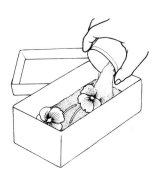

Drying with dessicant

Silica gel, available from a large florist or gardening
centre, is one of the best dessicants for drying plant
material. You can also use borax or a mixture of sand
and borax. Dessicants can be used over and over
again.

First, pour a layer of dessicant into a container, such
as a shoe box or a tin (the container must eventually
be made airtight). Place the plant material carefully
on top. Pour more dessicant over until the material is
completely buried. Put the lid on and leave for two or
three days. Be very careful when you remove the
fragile dry material.

Flowers to dry in Dessicant

Daffodil, Rose, Dahlia, Narcissus, Daisy, Cornflower,
Pansy, Chrysanthemum.
Try experimenting with other flowers and keep a
record of successes and failures!

Preserving with Glycerine

This method works particularly well with sprays of

leaves such as Oak and Beech. The leaves turn to beautiful autumnal browns and golds and make excellent background material for flower arrangements.

Pour a bottle of glycerine into a large glass jar and add twice as much hot water. Stand the sprays in the jar with between two and four inches of the stem in the solution. When all of the leaves have changed colour you can take the stems out.

Preserving in glycerine

Plant Material to Preserve in Glycerine

Leaves - Oak, Beech, Box, Broom, Laurel, Ivy, Rhododendron, Pittosporum

Flowers - Hydrangea, Sea Holly

Seedheads - Foxglove, Iris, Snapdragons

A flower press

Pressing

Flower presses can be bought, or you can simply use a large, thick book. Place the material between the pages and put some other heavy books on top. It will probably take about four weeks for the flowers to dry, but if you want to use them for pictures it is better to leave them for about six months.

Pressing in a book

Plants for Pressing

Flowers - Daisies, Buttercups, Forget-Me-Nots, Honeysuckle

Leaves - Ferns, Maple, Oak, Beech

45

A card made with pressed flowers.

Summer Recipes

A selection of traditional, old-fashioned recipes to make use of the products of your flower garden and to enable you to enjoy its flavours and scents all through the year.

Rose Petal Vinegar

Fill a jam jar with rose petals. Then pour on them as much white vinegar as the jar will hold, cover it and stand it in the sun or other warm place for three weeks. Strain through a flannel bag and bottle for use.

Excellent for salads and other purposes.

Potpourri

Gather any scented flowers and leaves, such as Roses, Lavender, Verbena, Scented Geranium, Sweet Briar, Bay Leaves, Balm, etc. Pull the petals from large flowers and the heads from small ones. Spread all out on trays or sheets of white paper and put in the sun to dry. When quite dry, weigh the flowers, and to each ¼ lb., add 2 oz. each of bay salt and common salt, 1oz. of powdered Orris Root and ¼oz. of powdered Cloves and Cinnamon mixed.

Put the mixture into a large jar; keep closely covered and stir every day for the first three weeks. When thoroughly mixed, add a few drops of oil of Bergamot and oil of Cloves. If possible add some dried blossoms of Calycanthus, which is Allspice.

Potpourri can be packed in jars for storage, or left in open bowls to delicately scent your room. It releases its perfume more strongly if put in a warm place.

ELDER FLOWER

Rhubarb and Elderflower Jam

2 lemons

6lb. rhubarb

6lb. sugar

2 large handfuls elderflowers

Cut up Rhubarb into small pieces, place in a large bowl. Tie the petals of the Elderflowers in a muslin bag and place in the middle of the Rhubarb.

Cover with the Rhubarb and add the sugar. Place a board and cloth over the bowl and leave for 24 hours, stirring after the first 12 hours. Put into a preserving pan and heat gradually, but do not boil. Pour back into bowl for 24 hours more. Lift out the bag with the Elderflowers and add the juice and grated rind of the lemons. Put into preserving pan and boil until it sets.

Elderflower "Champagne"

2 heads Elderflower in full bloom

8 pt. cold water

1½lb. sugar

1 lemon

2 tablespoons wine vinegar

Squeeze juice of lemon. Cut rind in four and put with all the other ingredients in a large vessel and pour on the cold water. Steep 24 hours, strain into screw-topped bottles and keep for a fortnight, when it is ready to drink.

(Take care. This can be very fizzy indeed!)

Caper Sauce

1 oz. butter

1 oz. flour

½ pt. milk

salt and pepper

1-2 tablespoons chopped Capers
or preserved Nasturtium seeds.

Melt butter. When it is foaming add the flour and cook for 1 minute,
stirring frequently. Gradually stir in the rest of the milk. Add chopped
Capers and a dash of the spiced vinegar.

Preserved Nasturtium Seeds

(A substitute for Capers)

Wash Nasturtium seeds in cold water and soak overnight in cold
salted water.
Cover with cold spiced vinegar made by adding 2oz.
salt, a dozen peppercorns, a small piece of horse radish, 2 cloves and
3 or 4 tarragon leaves to each quart of vinegar. Seal and keep for
twelve months before using. Use these 'Capers' to liven up a pizza,
by scattering a few over the topping, or make 'Caper' sauce to eat
with lamb.

Flower Arranging

Arranging flowers successfully really isn't as difficult as it looks. Many people think that it is a specialised art requiring skill and training. But often, the simplest arrangements are the most effective. Rules, after all, are made to be broken, and you will probably find that most of the time the flowers will arrange themselves. A large bunch of Sweet Peas, for example, looks lovely when informally arranged in a plain white vase.

A few accessories are helpful, but the most important items are the flowers themselves.

Containers
You don't need a vast collection of vases, pots and urns. Just a few containers in different shapes and sizes are sufficient.

It is important to match the container to the type of flowers you are using for the arrangement. This sounds obvious, but quite often long stemmed flowers are pushed carelessly into short, dumpy vases, and small, delicate flowers swamped in vast bowls.

Instant containers can be made by painting yoghurt pots or empty tin cans, and even a plastic bucket can be used at a pinch. Glass tumblers make good containers for mixed summer posies.

Supports
You will need some form of 'anchor' to stop your arrangement from collapsing into an untidy heap, and to provide a weight to make lightweight containers more stable.

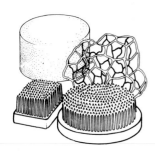

Metal Pin-Holders come in many shapes and sizes. Select one to fit your vase, anchor it firmly with a piece of plasticine and use it to spike individual flower stems.

Oasis is a light, plastic foam that soaks up water making it heavy and solid. Make sure it has soaked up as much water as possible. Place it on the bottom of the container and push the flower stems into it.

Chicken wire, cut roughly to the size of the container and crumpled up, can also be used to hold an arrangement in place.

SWEET PEA

Making an Arrangement

First, you should decide on the *style* of arrangement. This may well depend on the plant material available. For example, do you want a simple arrangement with just a few flowers? Or, do you want to create a spectacular display using a mass of flowers? The latter will require more time and skill!

It is also important to give a bit of thought to the overall colour of the arrangement. Bright, vibrant reds and yellows will give a warm look, where blues and whites will look cool.

The traditional Japanese style of flower arranging – Ikebana – uses a minimum of plant material but the effect is often stunning in its simplicity. At the other end of the scale, flower arrangements used to decorate churches may have hundreds of flowers.

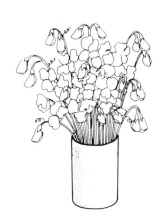

The finished arrangement must fit in with its setting. The size must be right – not too big, not too small, and the colours should not clash with their surroundings – unless you do this deliberately!

The shape of the final arrangement is also important. It is sometimes helpful to use a geometrical outline as a guide. Start by defining the shape with a few tall stems and then fill in the space between them. Arrangements can be either symmetrical or asymmetrical – round, crescent-shaped or triangular.

Making Flowers Last

Flower arrangements often take a lot of time and effort. So, it is very disappointing if the flowers immediately wilt and die. You can, of course, replace the odd one or two, but not an entire arrangement. There are a number of precautionary steps you can take to avoid such a disaster.

✳ Never pick flowers during the hottest part of the day. Early morning is best when the dew has dried off.

✳ Keep flowers in a shady place as you pick them.

✳ Use secateurs or scissors rather than tearing the stems with your hands.

✳ Put woody stems into water immediately and let them have a long drink before arranging.

✳ Cut woody stems under water. This eliminates any air locks and allows the sap to rise.

✳ Plunge stems of Roses into boiling water before arranging. But be careful to protect the flower heads by covering loosely with a polythene bag.

✳ Instant revival techniques include an aspirin dissolved in the water; a teaspoon of sugar; or a proprietary additive.

✳ Remove leaves from the lower part of the stem. This prevents them from decaying and fouling the water. *All* leaves should be removed from Lilac and Orange Blossom to prevent wilting.

✳ Roses can be preserved for special occasions by putting them in a polythene bag in the bottom of the fridge.

Useful Flowers to Grow

Chrysanthemums and Dahlias The spiky and pom-pom varieties are useful for autumn arrangements when there is little colour around.

Gladioli, Delphiniums and Hollyhocks These tall, elegant flowers are particularly useful for large, formal arrangements.

Gypsophila and London Pride The delicate, feathery flowers make good background material for arrangements.

Hosta The fleshy leaves of the plain and variegated varieties provide excellent foliage for arrangements.

Ivy The long, trailing strands are useful for outlining arrangements.

Holly The more berries the better. Good for Christmas decorations.

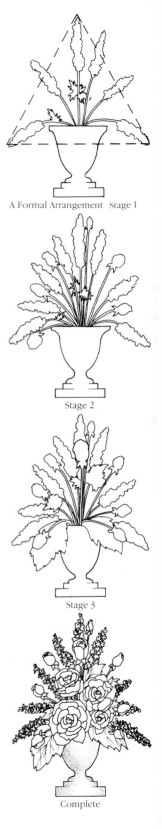

A Formal Arrangement Stage 1

Stage 2

Stage 3

Complete

Planting a Wild Garden

And in the warm hedge grew lush eglantines,
  Green cow-bind and the moonlight-coloured
  may,
And cherry blossoms, and white cups whose wine
  Was the bright dew yet drained not by the Day;
And wild roses, and ivy serpentine,
  With its dark buds and leaves wandering astray;
Percy Bysshe Shelley

Sadly, hundreds of species of wild flowers are in danger of disappearing for good; chemical sprays, farm machinery and new building sites threaten their natural habitats.

There are laws to protect over 60 species, and you are not allowed to dig up *any* flowers that are growing wild without the permission of the landowner.

However, there is nothing to stop you from gathering seeds and starting your own wild garden. By doing this you will be playing an important role in the conservation of wild plants and animals too.

Choose a neglected spot – a part of your own garden, or a quiet patch of woodland or meadowland (you will need permission for the latter). If there is a stream running through, or a pond, so much the better.

Scatter seed at random and plant clumps of bulbs – Narcissi, Snowdrops, Scillas, and Hyacinths. Bulbs for growing in the garden will soon revert to their natural state if left untouched.

Let the weeds grow. You can tidy them up a bit if they threaten to strangle other plants, but some have very pretty flowers. And Nettles are a great attraction to butterflies.

Your secluded garden will be a perfect haven for many small creatures – mice, voles, spiders, beetles, squirrels, birds and butterflies.

Keep a month-by-month record, sketching or photographing the flowers and wildlife. You will be amazed at how quickly your wilderness will spread.

The following are some suggestions for plants to grow in a natural setting, but the list is endless. Some seed merchants sell packets of mixed wild flower seeds.

Poppy, Dandelion, Buttercup, Campanula, Violet, Foxglove, Clover, Ivy, Celandine, Lady's Smock, Feverfew, Cowslip, Oxlip, Meadow Sweet, Nettle, Thistle, Balm, Catmint, Valerian, Bog Myrtle, Creeping Jenny, Periwinkle. *By water:* Iris, Fern, Hosta, Primrose, Rush, Marsh Marigold.

RED CLOVER

Friends and Enemies in the Garden

He crawleth here. He creepyth there
*   On lyttel cat-like feet.*
He weareth coats of gorgeous fur
*   And lyveth but to eat.*

He gnaweth lettuce into shreddes
*   And, burrowing with his nose,*
He tattereth half the garden beddes
*   And fretteth e'en the rose.*

Alfred Noyes

Gardeners should always be on the look out for tell-tale signs of enemy action – withered and yellowing leaves, neatly scissored stems and flowers peppered with tiny holes.

Chemical sprays, powders and pellets have their uses but in most cases 'prevention is better than cure'. You can discourage pests by keeping the garden clean and tidy – removing debris and weeding regularly. You can also enlist the help of some of nature's friends.

Garden Enemies

The following list includes some of the better-known trouble makers, together with a few gardener's friends.

S*lugs* damage leaves, stems and flowers. They leave a slimy trail behind them and are most active at night and after rain. Poisoned slug pellets are effective, but they should be placed under a tile, or the hollowed-out shell of a grapefruit, to stop birds from eating them. An old remedy is to sprinkle slugs' tails with salt.

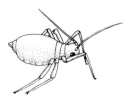

A*phids* include greenflies and blackflies. They multiply at an alarming rate and do untold damage by sapping juices from stems and leaves. Plants should be sprayed with insecticide as soon as aphids are spotted.

C*aterpillars* have voracious appetites. They leave gaping holes in leaves. Spraying is probably the only solution.

Ants cause damage to plant roots. Their vigorous burrowing loosens the soil around the roots and plants often die as a result. Ants also help to spread greenflies, carrying them bodily from plant to plant. Boiling water is often sufficient to get rid of a nest, or simply digging the soil. If this fails, special dust can be used.

E*arwigs* have a nasty habit of devouring Dahlias and Chrysanthemums. If you spot one, shake it off and get rid of it immediately!

M*ice* nibble and gnaw away at bulbs. If you cannot bear the thought of traps, try surrounding your bulbs with prickly leaves.

Garden Friends

B*ees* carry pollen from flower to flower ensuring that successful pollination takes place.

L*adybirds* help by eating greenflies.

E*arthworms* are invaluable for their help in breaking up the subsoil and carrying humus from the surface to where it is needed.

T*oads* may look ugly but they do good work by eating all the slugs in sight.

B*irds* are both friends and foes. Robins and Blue Tits, in particular, eat greenflies and caterpillars, but they are also partial to tender young shoots. Thrushes eat slugs and snails. Sparrows peck and tear off yellow spring flowers such as Crocuses and Primulas, and Bullfinches can be a menace in orchards, gobbling up the flower buds on the fruit trees. Protect yellow flowers with a network of black cotton and hang shining and rattling objects in your fruit trees to keep these birds away.

Butterflies

As butterflies are but winged flowers,
Half sorry for their change, who fain,
So still and long they lie on leaves,
Would be thought flowers again –
William Henry Davies

There are about 70 different species of butterflies in the British Isles, but only a few are regular garden visitors.

You may have wondered why some gardens are full of brightly-coloured butterflies, while others have none at all. A great deal depends on which flowers and shrubs are on offer! Butterflies need a plentiful supply of nectar so they are much more likely to frequent gardens where there is an abundant supply of flowers.

To make sure of having butterflies in your garden, try planting a **Buddleia**. The species **Buddleia Davidii** – the butterfly bush – has purple spikes of flowers and long, pointed leaves. It grows to about 12 ft. in height. To keep the Buddleia strong and bushy, prune new shoots hard back in March.

For quicker results, sow seeds of **Valerian** between April and June. Butterflies love the heavy clusters of pink, red and white star-shaped flowers, smelling strongly of Jasmine. The following butterflies are among the most common visitors.

Small Tortoiseshell Female has reddish brown wings with dark 'tortoise-shell' markings and blue spots on wing tips. Found early spring and autumn. Fond of Michaelmas Daisies, Nettles and Thistles.

Red Admiral Female has scarlet bands with white markings on front wings and scarlet bands with black spots on back wings. Found from June to early October.

Peacock Both male and female have beautiful eye spots on front and back wings. Found late July to end September. Eggs are laid on underside of Nettle leaves.

Large White The scourge of all keen vegetable gardeners! Lays eggs on cabbage leaves. Found April to June. Dark markings on front wings (female has eye spots on front wings).

MICHAELMAS DAISY

Cures and Remedies

His Aunt Jobiska made him drink
Lavender water tinged with pink,
For she said, 'The world in general knows
There's nothing so good for a Pobble's toes!'
Edward Lear

Did you realise that your garden could double as a medicine cabinet and a beauty parlour? Some people are convinced that certain plants have healing properties. Others are highly suspicious of claims that plants can be used to cure ailments ranging from sore throats and headaches to sprains and stomach pains. There can be little doubt, though, that it is more pleasant to sip a soothing herbal drink than swallow a couple of pills.

Plant extracts can also be used externally. Rosewater, for example, makes a wonderful skin freshener. Many cosmetics sold in shops are based on plant products, but you can make your own quite easily!

The following are just a few of the remedies, lotions and potions based on plant materials. Where an *infusion* is recommended, simply pour boiling water over the leaves or flowers suggested. Drink, or apply, when pleasantly warm, but do not allow to steep too long.

Rosewater can only be made by a process of distillation. You can make your own at home by adding 1 oz. essence of roses (from good chemists) to 1 gallon distilled water. Mix well and leave for a week or more.

Put 4 oz. dry **Lavender** flowers in a jar with a lid. Add ½ pt. cider vinegar and leave in a dark place for 1 – 2 weeks. Shake jar each day. Strain into a clean bottle and add ¼ pt. Rosewater. Dabbed onto the temples, this sweet-smelling lotion may ease tension and relieve headaches.

Pour about ½ pt. of boiling water over some sprigs of **Rosemary**. Leave until warm. Use to rinse dark hair after washing. It will leave hair shiny and enhance the colour. For fair hair, use **Chamomile** flowers.

Mix a good handful of dried **Mint, Thyme** and **Marjoram** with ½ pt. each of mild vinegar and water. Add to your bath water for an instant 'lift'.

To soothe a sore throat, make an infusion with **Borage** leaves and sip slowly.

Rub **Dock** leaves on rash caused by stinging nettles. **Mint** leaves can also be used to relieve the irritation.

Insect bites can be made less irritating by rubbing gently with a **Marigold** leaf.

An infusion of **Fennel** is said to be a good cure for the common cold.

AUTUMN

Sing a song of seasons!
Something bright in all!
Flowers in the Summer,
Fires in the Fall.

Robert Louis Stevenson

As the leaves turn from green to pale gold, and finally to deep red, purple and brown, the days begin to close in – autumn has arrived. The first early morning frosts threaten late blooms and winds begin to bite.

There is still a good deal of life in the garden though, with autumnal colours predominating. Chrysanthemums and Dahlias are at their best, but they need protecting from the frequent gusting gales. Other late flowers include Michaelmas Daisies, Zinnias, Autumn Crocuses, Red Hot Pokers and Montbretia.

Autumn is a busy time for gardeners: tidying up borders, raking leaves and windfalls, and stoking endless bonfires.

With the hardening of the ground, birds find it increasingly difficult to find food. You can help by stepping up the supply of food – bread, bacon rinds, pieces of fat and nuts. Some garden centres sell special seed for wild birds. But make sure that the food is out of reach of cheeky squirrels – they should be building up their own larder!

MOUNTAIN ASH

Jobs in Your Garden
in Autumn

Season of mists and mellow fruitfulness.
Close bosom-friend of the maturing sun.

John Keats

The Lawn

By October you will not need to mow as frequently as in the summer months. The blades of the mower can now be raised by about a ¼ inch. Keep the lawn clear of dead leaves by raking with a springy rake or brushing with a twiggy 'besom'. If you have space in the garden, pile up the leaves in a heap so they can rot down into leaf mould to fertilise the garden next spring. Aerate the lawn with a fork, as in the summer, and apply an autumn fertiliser. Disperse any worm casts. They could cause bald patches on the lawn and so encourage weeds.

Annuals

From September onwards your annuals will be fading and can be dug up to make way for the planting of bulbs for spring. In mild southerly areas, the seeds of hardy annuals can be sown, to flower next year (see page 34).

Biennials

Sweet Williams, Forget-Me-Nots and Wall Flowers can be planted out, ready to flower in the spring. Water them in well.

Bulbs

Daffodils, Snowdrops and Crocuses should be planted in September, Hyacinths and Tulips in October. Try planting groups of Snowdrops and Crocuses on your lawn. Their foliage should have died down before the lawn is mown in spring. Most bulbs look best planted in informal groups. To achieve a natural effect, scatter a handful of bulbs gently over the area you wish to plant and plant them where they fall. The correct depth for planting is usually at twice the depth of the bulb itself. September is the month to start planting bulbs in pots and bowls to bloom indoors at Christmas (see page 77).

Lily bulbs should be planted in autumn and winter, from October onwards. Plant them in a sheltered corner at twice to three times the depth of the bulb. Lilies give such a spectacular display that they look difficult to grow, but in fact they are surprisingly easy.

Roses

Continue to spray the Roses to protect them from disease –
particularly mildew which is especially prevalent at this time of year.
Train in long shoots on climbers and ramblers and tie them so that
they don't get battered by strong autumn winds. Rake up and burn
fallen Rose leaves to help prevent diseases recurring next year.

The Herbaceous Border

October is the month to plant new hardy perennials and shrubs. After
the first frosts have blackened the foliage of Dahlias, cut back the
foliage, dig up the tubers carefully, dry them and store them away for
the winter. Chrysanthemums and Gladioli can be lifted and stored
now, too.

Diary for September

Warm September brings the fruit,
Sportsmen then begin to shoot.

BLACKBERRY

Diary for October
Fresh October brings the pheasant,
Then to gather nuts is pleasant.

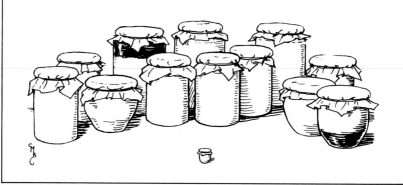

Diary for November

Dull November brings the blast,
Then the leaves are whirling fast.

Shrubs with Berries

Autumn is the best time to plant shrubs, but it's also the moment to enjoy the cheerful displays of brightly coloured berries on established shrubs and trees.

Most of the plants described on this page come into their full glory in autumn, when their rather inconspicuous flowers give way to the reds and golds of berries and autumn foliage.

The *Spindle* (Eonymus) shown in the picture has distinctive fruits, like little red lanterns, splitting open to reveal orange seeds. It is a hardy shrub or small tree, growing to no more than 10 ft. high.

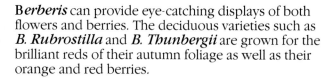

B*erberis* can provide eye-catching displays of both flowers and berries. The deciduous varieties such as *B. Rubrostilla* and *B. Thunbergii* are grown for the brilliant reds of their autumn foliage as well as their orange and red berries.

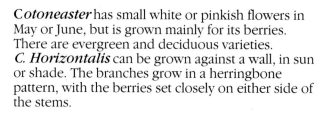

C*otoneaster* has small white or pinkish flowers in May or June, but is grown mainly for its berries. There are evergreen and deciduous varieties. *C. Horizontalis* can be grown against a wall, in sun or shade. The branches grow in a herringbone pattern, with the berries set closely on either side of the stems.

P*yracantha* (Firethorn) is a hardy evergreen to grow as a hedge or against a wall, where it will need the support of a trellis. It has creamy white flowers, like a hawthorn, followed by copious clusters of orange or red berries which last right through the winter. It will tolerate sun or partial shade.

There are *Viburnums* to suit many different purposes in the garden, including autumn colour. *V. Betulifolium* is deciduous with dark green leaves, white flowers in May or June and clusters of red berries in the autumn. You'll need patience because it won't produce berries for the first few years. *V. Davidii* is evergreen, low growing and good for ground cover. It likes moist conditions and should be grown in an open, sunny position. Male and female bushes have to be planted together if they are to produce their greenish-blue berries.

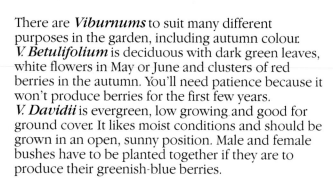

SPINDLE BERRY

Autumn Recipes

Many of the plants which we have recommended for your flower garden also bear fruits. Here are some recipes which make use of those fruits.

Crab Apple Jelly

Crab Apples

Sugar

Wash and cut up crab apples. Boil until quite soft. Strain through a jelly bag. To 1 pt. of juice add 1 lb. of sugar. Boil quickly till it sets. Pour into hot pots and seal.

Rose and Perfumed Jellies

A good crop of crab apples means plenty of jelly, but so often this also spells monotony. But it need not. It makes the finest base for a preserve of your favourite perfume from the garden or flavour from the herb garden.

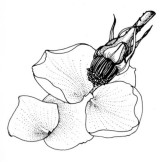

For *Rose Jelly*, which some find so much more palatable than the syrupy conserve usually made from rose petals, pound down a quantity of strongly perfumed fresh rose petals with caster sugar so that the sugar absorbs the juice from the crushed petals. Cover with the smallest quantity of water and stew gently in a covered dish in the oven. Strain and add to the crab apple jelly and boil up.

This method can be followed with scented geranium leaves, verbena, mint and peppermint, the small stems of angelica which are too small to crystallize can also be used, only as the spring is the time for angelica, you must keep some jelly from the previous autumn or use gooseberry jelly.

Jelly Making Hints

Cook fruit slowly. Place in muslin jelly bag over bowl and leave to drain. Leave pulp to drain 24 hours without pressing. Bring strained juice to boil before adding sugar. Sugar should be stirred until it is dissolved. Test for set after 10 minutes' quick boiling. Careful skimming at the end is necessary to obtain a clear jelly.

Japonica Jam

4 lb. Japonica fruit

7 pt. water

1 heaped teaspoon powdered cloves

Sugar

Wash fruit, cut into eighths. Boil with water until tender and then sieve. Weigh the pulp, add equal weight of sugar, stir and bring to boil. Add powdered spice. Boil for 10 minutes, test in a plate for setting, pot and cover at once.

Sloe Gin

This recipe is adaptable to whatever quantity of sloes you are able to gather from your garden or a hedgerow.

Wash the sloes and prick them to release their juice. Pile them into a glass jar. Pour in enough granulated sugar to fill the spaces between the sloes, shaking it down once or twice. Fill to the brim with gin and seal the jar. By Christmas, the Sloe Gin should be ready to decant and drink.

Plants For Shady Places

There are a number of plants – not of the 'hot house' variety – that thrive in dark, shady corners. Most of them are fairly hardy and can be left to their own devices. Try to choose bright colours where possible so that the flowers stand out from their gloomy surroundings.

P*eriwinkle* (Vinca) with blue flowers and green or variegated leaves provides good ground cover in shady areas.

F*oxgloves* Plant between October and April in partial shade. Cut off the central flower spike after flowering to encourage side shoots.

F*erns* There are over 100 species of ferns, all of which thrive in shady spots. The graceful, green fronds are useful in flower arrangements. Plant in March and April. Divide existing crowns in April.

B*luebells,* also known as ***Wild Hyacinths,*** grow in shady woods but can equally well be grown in flower beds. In spite of the name, they also come in white and pink varieties.

I*vy* grows practically anywhere and provides excellent ground cover. It can also be trained up a wall to disguise ugly brickwork and drain-pipes. Plant between September and March. Cuttings can be taken at the end of summer. The variegated varieties are particularly attractive with their pale outer frill and inner core of dark green.

S*cillas* have dainty blue flowers with shiny leaves. Plant bulbs from late summer to early autumn. Prefer partial shade and a well-drained soil.

P*rimulas* are useful for bringing bright splashes of colour to borders early in the year. Prefer damp soil that does not dry out. Plant between autumn and spring. Divide after flowering and plant in position for following year.

R*hododendrons* come into their own in late spring when they are a mass of colourful blooms. There are many different varieties – from dwarf to tree height. Prefer a shady position in well-drained soil. Rhododendrons are lime haters.

PERIWINKLE

Planting Bulbs

As summer draws to a close it's time to start planning for a display of spring bulbs indoors and out.

In the Garden

A bulb planter

Most bulbs look their best in informal groups in borders, on lawns, among trees and on banks and rockeries. To achieve an informal effect, take a handful of bulbs and scatter them over a small area. Then plant them where they fall. On lawns a bulb planter is a very useful tool for digging holes for larger bulbs, such as Daffodils. It removes a neat plug of turf which can be replaced on top of the bulb. Holes for smaller bulbs such as Crocuses can be made with a large stick. Fill up the hole with soil after planting the bulb and the grass will soon grow to cover the small bald patch.

As a general rule, bulbs need to be covered with twice their depth of soil. The chart below gives a general guide to planting the bulbs mentioned on pages 18 and 19. Depth of planting means the depth of soil above the top of the bulb.

	When to Plant	Depth of Planting (inches)	Distance Apart (inches)
Allium	Sept-Oct	3-4″	4-6″
Crocus	Aug-Oct	2″	3″
Fritillaries: Snake's Head	Sept-Oct	4-6″	4-6″
Crown Imperial	Sept-Oct	8″	9-15″
Grape Hyacinth	Sept-Oct	2-3″	2-3″
Hyacinth	Oct-Nov	4-5″	6″
Lily of the Valley	Sept-Oct	Just below surface	6-8″
Narcissus (including Daffodils)	Aug-Sept	4-5″	4-6″
Scilla	Aug-Sept	2-3″	2-3″
Snowdrop	Aug-Sept	2″	3-6″
Tulip	Oct-Nov	4-5″	6″

Indoors

It's possible to buy bulbs specially prepared for 'forcing' indoors. If these are not available, use the largest, plumpest bulbs you can find. Not all bulbs can be successfully grown in this way, but Hyacinths, Daffodils, Tulips and some of the small bulbous Irises will reward you with midwinter colour in your home.

Choose a bowl or pot that is deep enough for the bulbs to have plenty of room for their roots. If there is a hole at the bottom of the pot, cover it with crocks and a layer of peat to help drainage. You can use potting compost in this sort of pot, but for an ornamental bowl with no hole you will need to use bulb fibre.

First soak the fibre, then squeeze out the excess water and cover the bottom of the bowl with a layer of fibre deep enough to bring the tops of the bulbs level with the rim of the bowl. Stand the bulbs on the fibre as close together as possible, but not touching, and fill up the bowl with fibre, leaving the tips of the bulbs above the surface.

Store the filled bowls in a cool dark place. Indoors, you can wrap them in newspaper to keep out the light. Out-of-doors, 'plunge' them under a layer of peat or soil 6 inches deep.

Eight to ten weeks later the bulbs should have finished establishing roots and can be brought into the light, but don't bring them into a warm room until the flower buds are beginning to show above the bulbs. If you plant several bowls at intervals of a few weeks, you should have a succession of flowers to brighten up the winter.

Cover base of bowl with fibre.

Stand bulbs on fibre.

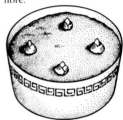
Leave tops of bulbs above fibre.

WINTER

Silly gardener! Summer goes,
  And winter comes with pinching toes,
When in the garden bare and brown
  You must lay your barrow down.

Robert Louis Stevenson

Even when the snow is thick on the ground, and the wind is howling down the chimney, there will still be something in the garden that needs attention. A gardener's work is never done!

By the time winter really sets in, the garden should be looking neat and tidy, and probably quite bare. But with a bit of advance planning, you should be able to have some colour around to relieve the gloom. Evergreens are an obvious example, and hardy heathers give a wonderful range of hues, from pink to white and gold. Some species of Rhododendrons, Camellias and Viburnums will flower round about Christmas, and brilliant, yellow Forsythia shortly afterwards.

Dried flower arrangements can take the place of cut flowers, and festive wreaths and decorations made from Holly, Pine sprays and Fir cones.

Keep up the supply of food to birds, and look out for hedgehogs that may have found a cosy corner in your shed or garage to snuggle up for winter. Don't disturb them, they will sleep right through to Spring.

HOLLY

Jobs in Your Garden in Winter

The cure for this ill is not to sit still,
Or frowst with a book by the fire;
But to take a large hoe and a shovel also,
And dig till you gently perspire.

Rudyard Kipling

The winter months are the time for tidying up in the garden and for planning ahead for next year.

The Lawn

The lawn mower can be stored away, cleaned and oiled. Untidy edges can be neatened and worn patches repaired by cutting turves and turning them round so that the balder areas are moved to a place where they will suffer less wear and tear.

Annuals

While away the dull winter evenings by browsing through colourful seed catalogues and planning a planting scheme for next spring. In February, the first of the half-hardy annuals can be sown in seed trays indoors. If you have not already dug the flower beds in preparation for spring planting, now is the time to do it. Dig in some manure or compost, too.

General

Tidy beds and borders and dig between the perennials. Make sure that your perennials are labelled. You will lose sight of them in midwinter when their dead growth has been cleared away and it's all too easy to forget their exact position! Check over stored Dahlia tubers, Gladiolus corms and Chrysanthemums. After heavy snow falls, knock snow off the branches of fragile shrubs and young trees. Bring out the bulbs you have 'forced' for Christmas, and enjoy a break from gardening. The hard work will soon start again!

Diary for December

Chill December brings the sleet
Blazing fire and Christmas treat.

and January

January brings the snow,
Makes our feet and fingers glow.

Diary for February

February brings the rain,
Thaws the frozen lake again.

SNOWDROP

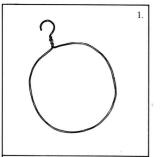

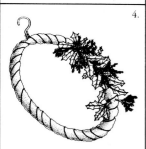

Christmas Decorations

The holly and the ivy,
When they are both full grown,
Of all the trees that are in the wood,
The holly bears the crown.

Traditional

Christmas wouldn't be the same without decorations – holly wreaths, Christmas trees, and colourful table arrangements. Leaves and flowers are in short supply at this time of year, but the traditional evergreens are all there.

Arm yourself with plenty of holly and any other available evergreen leaves, including pine branches and cones. Add to this some coloured balls, candles, ribbon and tinsel and you'll be ready to start.

Mistletoe is also very popular at this time of year. Try growing your own by rubbing ripe berries on the underside of young apple branches. The berries will attract the Mistle Thrush, so make sure you get to them first.

Christmas Wreath

1. Make a circular frame from thick wire or an old coat-hanger. **2.** Bind thick wads of moss to the frame using thin wire or twine. **3.** Soak the wreath in a bucket of water. **4.** Poke in pieces of holly and evergreen leaves to cover the moss. **5.** Attach a few coloured balls and wind a red ribbon round the wreath. It is now ready to hang on the outside of the door.

Christmas Tree

Tastes in decorating trees vary enormously. Some people prefer brightly coloured balls and tinsel, but a much simpler colour scheme can be very effective. Try using just gold and silver, or red and gold. Pine cones sprayed with gold and silver paint make simple, natural ornaments to hang on the tree. Choose a sturdy well-shaped tree that stands straight with no kinks or bends. If possible, buy one with roots so that you can plant it in the garden afterwards. Aerosol sprays are available that stop pine needles from dropping all over the carpet.

Table Decorations

1. Start with a piece of log about 9 inches long. Bore a hole in it, wide enough to take a candle. Spray the log with 'artificial' snow and decorate with sprigs of holly and sprays of pine. Add a few coloured balls. If the log won't stand still anchor it to a cake stand with pieces of plasticine.

2. Take a block of oasis about 5 inches square and push four or five white candles firmly into the top of it. Mask the oasis by pushing in sprays of holly leaves and trails of ivy sprayed with gold paint. Grains of gold or silver glitter or tiny gold stars shaken onto the leaves while the paint is wet will give the arrangement extra sparkle, and you can fill any gaps with gold balls left over from the Christmas tree.

Winter Colour

Through the gloomy winter months when most trees and flowerbeds are bare, it's still possible to have cheerful colours in your garden with winter-flowering shrubs, evergreens and bushes with brightly-coloured bark.

Winter Jasmine (Jasminus Nudiflorum) bears bright yellow trumpet-shaped flowers on its slender green branches from November right through to April. It will grow in almost any position, sunny or shady, supported by a wall, fence or trellis.

Witch Hazel has thick clusters of flowers like bunches of tiny ribbons on bare branches from January onwards, or even earlier. A popular variety is Hamamelis Mollis, a small tree with bright yellow flowers that are sweetly scented.

Another winter-flowering shrub is a variety of *Viburnum: Bodnantense Dawn.* Its white flowers, tinged with pink, are open from November until March.

For unusual bark colours try *Cornus Alba* (Dogwood). The bare, upright stems of this shrub can be a surprisingly bright red in winter.

There are many Winter-flowering varieties of *Erica.* Given an acid soil and a sunny, open position in a border or rockery, they will flower for months on end and need very little attention. *Helleborus* is a family of winter-flowering perennials of which the best-known member is the *Christmas Rose,* Helleborus Niger, whose white flowers with golden centres are borne from December to March. The flower buds may need protection from the heaviest winter frosts.

Around Christmas it's natural to think of the traditional evergreens, holly and ivy, but for added colour in winter, why not try some of the variegated kinds, with bright green leaves edged in yellow or white? And you can create marvellously subtle arrangements of different greens with a selection of low-growing juniper bushes. The colours of their foliage range from blue-green through to a bright yellowish green.

Whichever of these plants you choose it's wise to site them near the house so they can easily be viewed from a window if the weather is too cold or wet to tempt you outside.

WINTER JASMINE

Birds in the Garden

Birds are often regarded as pests in the garden – particularly when they leave prize blooms peppered with tiny holes. But many people are content to share their garden with birds and wild animals, and may even wish to encourage them!

During spring and summer birds are more or less self-sufficient. There are plenty of fat, juicy worms around and the ground is soft enough for birds to grub around in. You should not put any food out when the weather is fine as this will make the birds lazy. But you can help by providing a supply of water – particularly on very hot days.

A shallow dish makes a good make-shift bird bath. But don't use a tin dish as it will get too hot. Birds will have great fun flapping and splashing as well as drinking. For a more permanent fixture, you can buy a cement bird bath. The bowl should be about 2-3 inches deep and stand high enough to prevent other animals from getting at it. The edges should preferably be rough enough to give the birds a good grip.

As soon as the ground gets hard you can start putting food out. This is especially important when there is snow on the ground. A wooden tray supported on the end of a pole makes a good feeding table and keeps greedy squirrels and cats at bay. Favourite foodstuffs include lumps of fat, nuts, seeds, bread, coconut and even boiled rice and potatoes. Check that metal containers do not have any rough edges that may cause injuries.

You can encourage birds to nest in your garden by providing nesting boxes. A simple version can be made by nailing a small hollow log to a tree. Standard nesting boxes have four walls and a slanting roof. The size of opening varies depending on what type of bird you want to attract. The more natural the box looks, the better. Birds are fairly adept at finding their own nesting material, but you can help by providing a supply of pieces of string, cotton, twigs and hair. Boxes should be thoroughly cleaned out at the end of each nesting season.

Another way of attracting birds to the garden is to grow some of their favourite plants – Lilac, Honeysuckle, Marigolds, Asters and Zinnias. The plants won't look very pretty when the birds have finished with them, but it may keep them off your prize blooms.

Heralds of Spring

Once the Christmas festivities are over the gardener will be looking for the first signs of the approach of spring, and he shouldn't have long to wait.

One of the first flowers to brave the cold after the turn of the year is the *Winter Aconite.* By February, tubers planted at the end of the previous summer will have produced bright yellow flowers, like Buttercups with a circular collar of leaves. The flowers may appear even earlier in mild weather. When summer comes the flower stems and foliage will have died away to reappear the following year.

In a mild spell, the pretty pink or red flowers of the shrub *Japonica,* or Japanese Quince, may appear on bare twigs as early as January, and last right through to April when the leaves begin to unfold. In autumn, the Japonica bears edible greenish yellow fruits, similar to quinces, which can be used to make jam.

In the countryside some of the earliest heralds of spring are *Hazel* and *Willow* catkins. If you have room in your garden for small trees it would be worth considering both of these. The male flowers of the Hazel are like yellow lambs-tails dancing in the wind and the female flowers are tiny red tufts that go unnoticed unless you look closely at the twigs. For an Easter decoration, cut branches of Hazel twigs and hang them with decorated blown egg shells. This is a tradition in many European countries.

Willow Catkins are the well-known and loved 'Pussy Willows.' They are soft and furry and silvery-grey when they first appear, turning yellow when the pollen ripens. A Willow tree can be a very decorative feature in any garden and the weeping form is very popular. It will be one of the first trees to burst into leaf in your garden in the spring.

WINTER ACONITE

Useful Addresses

The Royal Horticultural Society, Vincent Square, London SW1P 2PE.

RHS Garden, Wisley, Woking, Surrey.

National Society of Allotment and Leisure Gardeners Ltd., 22 High Street, Flitwick, Bedfordshire, MK45 1DT.

Seed Catalogues

Samuel Dobie & Son Ltd., Upper Dee Mills, Llangollen, Clwyd, LL20 8SD.

S. E. Marshall & Co. Ltd., Regal Road, Wisbech, Cambs., PE13 2RF.

Suttons Seeds Ltd., Hele Road, Torquay, Devon, TQ2 7QJ.

Thompson & Morgan Ltd., London Road, Ipswich, Suffolk, IP2 0BA.

Unwins Seeds Ltd., Histon, Cambridge, CB4 4LE.

The Plant and Seed Club of Great Britain, 69 Lincoln Street, Wakefield, West Yorkshire.

Herb Specialists

Herbs by Post, The Barn, Wellesbourne Road, Moreton Morrell, Warwickshire, CV35 9OB.

Valeswood Herb Farm, Little Ness, Shrewsbury, Salop.

Oak Cottage Herb Farm, Nesscliffe, Salop, SY4 1DB.

Gardens to Visit

Bateman's, Burwash, Etchingham, East Sussex, TN19 7DS.

Rudyard Kipling's home from 1902-36. Garden with restored water-mill. Open: March to end September.

Bodnant, Tal-y-Cafn, Colwyn Bay, Gwynedd, LL28 5RE.

One of the finest gardens in the country with magnificent Rhododendrons, Camellias, Magnolias, shrubs and trees. Open: mid-March to end October.

Dunster Castle, Dunster, Nr Minehead, Somerset, TA24 6SL.

Terraced garden of rare shrubs in grounds of 13th-century castle. Open: April to October.

Great Gardens of England, Syon Park, Brentford, Middlesex.

Hidcote Manor Garden, Hidcote Bartrim, Chipping Campden, Gloucestershire.

Famous for rare shrubs, trees, herbaceous borders and *old* roses. Open: April to end October.

Nymans Garden, Handcross, Nr Haywards Heath, West Sussex, RH17 6EB.

Many rare species of shrubs and trees from all over the world. Open: April to end October.

Scotney Castle Garden, Lamberhurst, Tunbridge Wells, Kent, TN3 8JN

Romantic garden with ruins of 14th-century moated castle. Open: April to end October.

Sheffield Park Garden, Uckfield, East Sussex, TN22 3QX.

18th-century garden and lakes laid out by the famous designer Capability Brown. Particularly beautiful in autumn. Open: April to mid-November.

Sissinghurst Castle Garden, Sissinghurst, Nr Cranbrook, Kent, TN17 2AB.

Garden designed by Vita Sackville-West and her husband Sir Harold Nicolson. Beautiful throughout the year. Open: April to mid-October.

Stourhead, Stourton, Warminster, Wiltshire, BA12 6QH

18th-century garden with lakes and temples. Many rare trees and plants. Open: All year.